Contents

What's awake?

Some animals are awake when you go to sleep.

Animals that stay awake at night are **nocturnal**.

Bats are awake at night.

What are bats?

Bats are **mammals** that can fly.

baby bat

Mammals have **fur**.

Mammal babies drink milk from their mother's body.

What do bats look like?

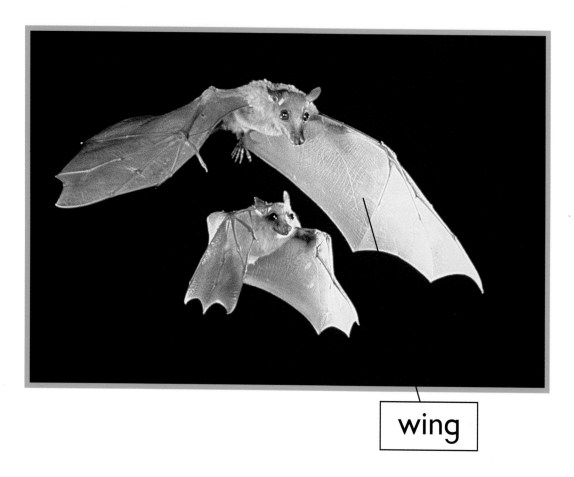

wing

Bats look like mice with big wings.

Their wings are covered with skin.

Some bats are as small as your hand.

Other bats have wings as wide as a man's arms.

Where do bats live?

Bats' homes are called **roosts**.

They live in groups called **colonies**.

In the wild, bats live in caves or trees.

In cities, bats live under **roofs** or bridges.

What do bats do at night?

Bats wake up just before dark.

They start to move around and fly a bit.

They fly away to look for food.

Bats can eat all night.

What do bats eat?

Most bats eat moths.

They eat other bugs, too.

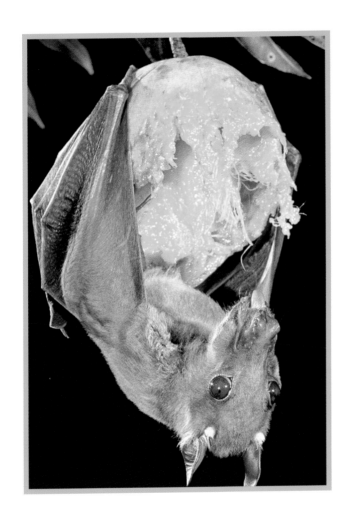

Many bats eat fruit.

This bat is eating a melon.

What do bats sound like?

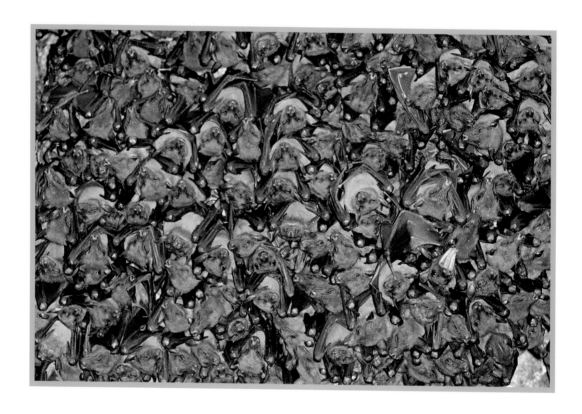

Bats make two kinds of noise.

One noise is a squeaking sound.

The other noise helps bats to
find food.

Scientists need to use machines
to hear this noise.

How are bats special?

Bats use a special noise to find bugs.

The sound bounces off the bugs, so the bat can tell where they are.

Bats hang upside down to sleep.

Where do bats go during the day?

In the morning, bats fly back to their **roosts**.

Bats take care of their babies.

Then they go to sleep.

Bat map

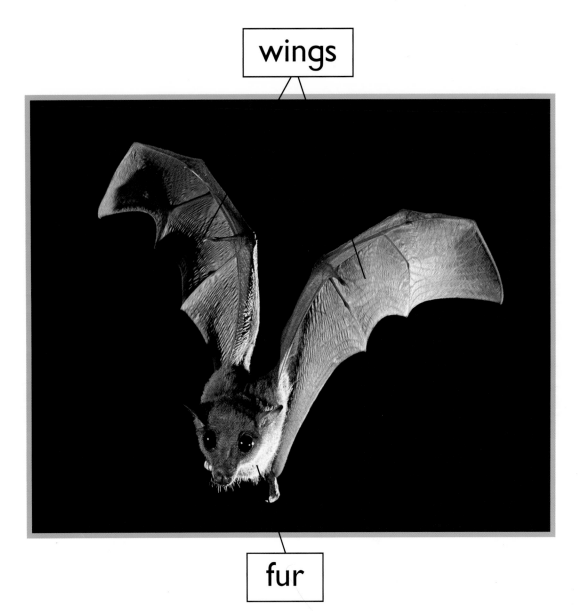

wings

fur

Glossary

colony
group of bats

fur
soft, short hair

mammal
animal that is covered in fur and feeds its babies with milk from its own body

nocturnal
awake at night

roof
part that covers the top of a house

roost
place where a bat colony lives

scientist
person who works to find out things about the world

Index